Gerhard Chroust
Petr Doucek
Lea Nedomová

25 Years of IDIMT
A History of Continuity
and Change

IDIMT

*Bibliografische Information der Deutschen Nationalbibliothek:
Die Deutsche Nationalbibliothek verzeichnet diese Publikation in der
Deutschen Nationalbibliografie;
detaillierte bibliografische Daten sind im Internet ueber
http://dnb.dnb.de abrufbar.*

*Herstellung und Verlag:
BoD - Books on Demand, Norderstedt, Deutschland
ISBN: 978-3-7448-0957-3*

Looking back at 25 years of IDIMT Conferences

The IDIMT Conferences were founded in 1993, soon after the fall of the Iron Curtain. This was one of the early scientific contacts which took place between Austria and the Czech Republic: A changed political situation, a new professor of Informatics at the Kepler University Linz, and a young promising and ambitious student at the the University of Economics Prague were the ingredients which promised a successful start for this series of conferences.

25 years are one generation in a human society and a long time in the fast-paced computer world. The IDIMT conferences have accompanied Information Management and Information Technology throughout these 25 years and have observed and commented dramatic changes and advances.

We began in 1993 in Kubova Hut', in a small South Bohemian village, with a mere 13 papers, 14 participants and 150 pages of proceedings. We now (2017) have 45 papers, 90 participants and almost 500 pages proceedings. We have undertaken made improvements and our conferences have consequently grown. IDIMT has proved to be a mirror of interests and trends in Information Management related business and research in Central Europe. Numerous persons have 'walked a part of this way with us' and have contributed to our success. Amongst many other factors, three main attributes defined the most essential points when IDIMT was founded:

- a loyal group of participants, who come year after year to present their findings and exchange information,

- the provision of ample discussion time after every session, considering the whole session and not a narrow view on a single paper,

- a friendly informal atmosphere and a group of participants to be easily known to one another.

The success has only been possible by the dedication and engagement of many of those persons taking over the key jobs.

This booklet is a modest attempt at recording of these eventful years. It is dedicated to all persons involved in participating and organizing the conferences. It presents in chronological order of all IDIMT conferences together with mentioning several small and large events, plus personal observations, some of which might even have escaped your attention. It includes photos of old friends and acquaintances.

At the end we also provide some summary data about the publications of the IDIMT conferences.

This booklet should also express a great THANK YOU to all of you who have helped to make the IDIMT conferences a success. It also attempts to induce you to keep interested in the future IDIMT Conferences.

We invite you to delve into the historical retrospective and enjoy some memories from past events.

Gerhard Chroust   Petr Doucek   Lea Nedomova

1 A new Conference is Born

1.1 "The times they are a-changin ..." (Petr Doucek remembers)

Let us look back at the past times when Europe was in a transition period: the Iron Curtain is breaking down and integration of the former political enemies - the Eastern socialist countries and the Western democratic countries - could start. We write 1991 when I received information about the possibility to perform my post-doc study in Austria with the support of the funding of the "Action Austria Czech Republic". The chance was to study with Professor Gerhard Chroust - the newly appointed head of the department of 'Systemtechnik und Automation' at the Johannes Kepler University in Linz. I started a two-month study assignment there and from that time I gained my first personal experience of academic habits, duties and manners, which are normally performed in the Western European countries and at their universities.

What was the general political and social climate in Europe at the beginning of the 90's? All Europe was excited by the fall of the Iron Curtain and all "modern Europeans" wanted to establish co-operations between the up to this time enemy blocks, without having to respect former borders between democratic and socialist countries. It was the time of getting to know one another - people from the eastern part of Europe wanted to know how the life was in the West and Western people wanted to visit formerly forbidden parts of their continent. This desire to get to know the other part of Europe occurred in different areas of human activities like travelling, business, and culture and at last but not at least academia, education, science and research and development framework.

The general frame of the Bologna process and conception of the European education is the fruit of this optimistic and enthusiastic period. Touristic visits are useful for knowing nature and buildings, but only few of the tourists are able to know, understand and accept specific features of the country where they stay. Usually they like to stay in n-stars hotels with comfortably equipped rooms, with international foods on the menu etc., but they have only few occasions to experience the touch and to feel the spirit of the country and the nation where they are on visit. When one wants to find a real long term partner for common work, be it for business, scientific or research and development work, one must visit the partner in his/her country and live there under her/his own conditions. This was the main reason, why I went to Austria to perform here my study assignment focusing on project management and software engineering.

1.2 IDIMT - From Prehistory to the Future (Petr Doucek continues)

My first feeling after arriving at the Johannes Kepler University at the department of 'Systemtechnik und Automation' was: there was, judged by ideas and flexibility, a very young, good working department with the charismatic boss with plenty of life energy. The main characteristic of Gerhard Chroust is - a lot of positive energy that he offers to all partners, students and staff of his department. He was the right engine, all time full of activity and every time prepared to support good ideas of his colleagues not only with advice, but also with concrete activities, large professional experience and a wisdom of life.

I finished my study at the Johannes Kepler University at the beginning of June 1992 and went back to Prague. At home, we discussed these results of my Austrian "trip" at our department meeting and came to the conclusion to form and to formulate a general proposal for a further common co-operation between these two departments. The best approach seemed to be in the form of a conference. The former head of the department and the vice-rector for research and development work at the University of Economics, Prague, professor Jan Ehleman supported this proposal. He arranged a visit to the Johannes Kepler University in the end of winter in 1992. Professor Gerhard Chroust as a co-founder of the co-operation accepted the proposal for a small conference type meetings and at this historical meeting in Linz all participants proclaimed common interests to work together and to start common research and development work. In this way, these founders built a new platform for co-operation between the Johannes Kepler University and the University of Economics, Prague. The real expression of this platform was to be in the form of a conference - the future IDIMT.

Key persons that contributed from the beginning of the IDIMT history were:

Professor Ernest Kulhavy: then Professor and University Representative for international contacts at the Johannes Kepler University Linz.

Prof. Jan Ehleman: , then Professor and Vice-Rector for international cooperation at the University of Economics Prague (fig. 3, fig. 14),

Professor Leo Vodáček (fig. 2), guru of management science at University of Economics, Prague and founder of the research discipline and master study program "Information management", the first guarantor of all courses of information management at Faculty of Informatics and Statistics.

Associate Professor Prokop Toman: University of Economics, Prague, the renaissance person, in majority focused on philosophical and social aspects of information system improvement in human community.

Fig. 3: Founders:G. Chroust, P. Doucek, J. Ehleman

Fig. 2: Leo Vodáček

We had to solve a lot of partial small and big questions and problems during this co-operation. The first of them were to find for our conference:

a location - main criteria for the conference choosing a location were:

- approximately the same distance from Linz and Prague - from this point of view we selected the first conference site in Kubova Hut' in the Šumava Mountains (Böhmerwald),

- convenient price level of the Czech Republic in comparison to Austrian - this aspect was and is up to this time, the reason why the conference is in the Czech Republic.

a name - the first year was run under the name "Information Management Workshop 1993". The programming and the organizing committee changed the name of the conference to "Interdisciplinary Information Management Talks" (IDIMT) in October 1993. This name is still valid and has been accepted up to our time - for 24 years!

Thanks to You all!
You were the first visionaries of IDIMT to an actual and future success !

1.3   Johannes Kepler University Linz, 1992 (Gerhard Chroust re-members)

In Spring 1992 I was serving my first few months as the newly appointed professor for Systems Engineering and Automation at the Kepler University. A young, talented, and very ambitious assistant from the University of Economics Prague had been awar-ded a two-month scholarship enabling him to study in Linz. I was informed by Prof. Dr. Ernest Kulhavy from the Kepler University Linz, who was in charge of intensifying external relationships, that this young man was going to spend his scholarship term at my institute. Prof. Kulhavy also suggested this to be the first step in establishing a close collaboration with the University of Economics Prague, where Prof. Dr. Jan Ehleman (fig. 3 and fig. 14), was in charge of external contacts. My Department of Systems Engineering and Automation in Linz (which then was part of the Institute of Systems Sciences) and the Department of Systems Analysis in Prague were to be the key con-tact points for this new collaboration. After a visit from colleagues from the University of Economics we agreed on starting a small bilateral conference in 1993 to establish and consolidate the cooperation. This suited me very well since I was, though no longer very young, only in my first year of professorship at the Kepler University. It presented itself as an important step towards academic cooperation. Petr Doucek offered his help and know-how in organizing the envisioned bi-lateral event in the Czech Republic.

In 1992/93 considerable differences in the economic situation and the political, econo-mic, and social environment existed between Austria and the Czech Republic. After the fall of the Iron Curtain the Czech Republic was actively striving to abolish the remainder of the old communist system.

Part of the challenge (and also the attraction) was that in many ways the two partners were of great difference: the Department of Systems Engineering and Automation of the Kepler University Linz was technology-oriented and the Department of Systems Analysis of the University of Economics was primarily economically oriented.

1.4   Bridging 25 years of IDIMT

Despite the long history of IDIMT we are proud to report that three of the 14 participants of the 1993 conference are still attending IDIMT conferences, as the attached Table of Contents of the 1993 Conference (Fig. 13) shows, together with the titles of their presentations.

Petr Doucek 1993: Comparing Software Process Model with Project Management Model
2017: Digital Economy (with Jakub Fischer, Ota Novotný)
Regulation of Cyber-Security in the Banking Sector (with Luděk Novák)
Short Journey Through 25 Years of IDIMT Conferences (with Gerhard Chroust and Lea Nedomová)

Gerhard Chroust 1993: Information Engineering
2017: Short Journey Through 25 Years of IDIMT Conferences (with Petr Doucek and Lea Nedomová)

Vlasta Svatá 1993: Information Management
2016: Use Cases for COBIT 5 Adoption

Fig. 4: The most faithful participants: G. Chroust, V. Svatá, P. Doucek

1.5   The 1993 Conference (Vlasta Svatá remembers)

Vlasta Svatá still recalls the first conference:

Despite the fact that it was 4 years after the Velvet Revolution, IDIMT 1993 was one of the first opportunity to meet colleagues from a "capitalist country" and to compare the level of knowledge in the area of IS/IT. As far as I remember I was very nervous, but the informal environment of the workshop and the friendly attitude of all the participants helped me to overcome these fears. From the professional point of view the workshop offered me the opportunity to verify my views on Information Management, which were partly different from my older colleagues and the management of the department. Contributions to the workshop have made me believe that the area of information management perceived in the context of a management style called IT Governance with a practical link to Corporate and Enterprise Governance has a great future. Developments in the coming years have confirmed these feelings.

Fig. 5: Vlasta Svatá

1.6   The locations of the IDIMT Conferences

The growing size and impact of the IDIMT conferences also went along with a change of location. Up to now 6 locations had hosted IDIMT conference, with respect to 2018 it looks like we will choose a seventh one.

Fig. 6: The six locations of IDIMT Conferences - 1993-2017 (Janie Chroust)

Kubova Hut', 1993-1994   The first phase of the IDIMT conference took place in Kubova Hut' in Šumava Mountains (Böhmerwald) in hotel Arnika in 1993. Kubova Hut' is a delightful little village near Boubin's wild forest in the heart of the Šumava Mountains, but with very poor accessibility. The conference was located here for two years.

Fig. 7: Kubova Hut' (Janie Chroust, 2000)

Zadov, 1995 - 2002 In 1995 a reconstruction of the Hotel Arnika started and we had to find a new location for the conference. The organizing committee moved the 1995 conference nearer to "civilization", to Zadov - a famous tourist and skiing center in the Šumava Mountains. The Zadov resort is approximately in the same distance from Prague as from Linz - 156 km. In Hotel Olympia, under the super-vision of Mr. Pavlik, the director of the hotel, the conference was held for eight years. The combination of professional service of the hotel staff, especially concerning catering and other supplementary needs plus beautiful scenery inspired the participants and influenced the spirit of the conference. During these eight years several innovations for the conference program were undertaken, more details can be found in Gerhard Chroust's paper [Chr07] and Petr Doucek's paper from 2006 [Dou06]. The session topics as well as the schema of the conference underwent considerable changes, see section 2.

Praha and Zadov, 2002 In 2002, on the tenth anniversary of the IDIMT meeting we added another important feature: The organizing committee decided to divide the conference into two parts. The first part was held in Prague and was organized for PhD students of the conference under the auspices of the former rector associate professor Jaroslava Duráková. She invited all participants to the private audience and to the cultural part of the PhD-day. Participants were able to visit the Charles University - the oldest University in the Middle Europe.

České Budějovice, 2003- 2007 In the same year (2003) an organizational problem developed in Hotel Zadov and the organizing committee moved the conference to České Budějovice - a historic city in South Bohemia (not to forget the famous beer!). Here we arranged the conference with the support of the theological faculty of the South Bohemian University. Center of the conference was the PVT hotel, which provided the accommodation and the conference room. Catering took place in Restaurant Metropol not far from the conference site.

Jindřichův Hradec, 2008 - 2012 The conditions in České Budějovice, especially accommodation, limited IDIMT's further development. Main problem was accommodation capacity - no more then 50 persons could an be accommodated in the

PVT hotel. The conference room only allowed 40 participants. So in 2008 the conference moved once more to a different location. This time we chose a city in which one of the faculties of the University of Economics, Prague, is located. Jindřichův Hradec was a very important city from 1200 to 1700. As a reminder of these times there is a beautiful market square and an impressive castle. 2008 we stayed in the Grand Hotel. In 2009 we moved to the larger hotel, the Hotel Concertino, just across the market square. This proved that the IDIMT conferences were flexible with respect to the location.

Praha, 2013 In 2013 we joined forces with the CONFENIS 2013 conference [BJNM13] in a joint and parallel conference in Prague at the University of Economics, Prague. We achieved some synergetic effects by listening to several lectures of the parallel conference, and we all had time to enjoy magnificent Prague, including a boat trip on the Moldawa.

Fig. 8: University of Economics Prague

Poděbrady, 2014 - ? In the following year (2014) we yet moved to a smaller, quieter place, to Poděbrady, founded in the 13th century and having considerable political importance in the 14th to 16th century. In 1905 a hot spring with carbonized water was detected and due to its stable weather and harmonious environment on the banks of the Elbe, and its well-maintained park it became an important Czech spa town. It still shows much of the atmosphere of the 1930's.

Fig. 9: Poděbrady, seen from the river Labe

1.7   The IDIMT Conferences 1993 - 2017

Jahr	authors	pagers	pages	Conference chairs and editors	Date of Conf	Location
1993	14	13	151	G. Chroust, P. Doucek	6.-8.Oct.	Kubova Huť
1994	27	23	233	same	9. 11.Nov..	same
1995	33	25	228	same	8.-10.Oct.	Zadov
1996	30	21	215	same	16.-18.Oct.	same
1997	35	30	320	S. Hofer, P. Doucek	15.-17.Oct.	same
1998	39	27	390	S. Hofer, M. Beneder	21.-23.Oct.	same
1999	46	34	424	same	02.-03.Sept.	same
2000	48	32	440	same	20.-22.Sept.	same
2001	45	29	397	C. Hofer, G. Chroust	19.-21.Sept.	same
2002	38	24	350	same	11.-13.Sept.	same
2003	38	24	310	same	10.-12.Sept.	České Budějovice
2004	31	23	304	same	15.-17.Sept.	same
2005	30	22	313	Ch. Hoyer, G. Chroust	14.-16.Sept.	same
2006	45	29	364	same	13.-15.Sept.	same
2007	38	27	383	Ch. Hoyer, G. Chroust, P. Doucek	12.-14.Sept.	same
2008	53	33	455	G. Chroust, P. Doucek, J. Klas	10.-12.Sept.	Jindřichův Hradec
2009	61	42	423	P. Doucek, G. Chroust, V. Oškrdal	9.-11.Sept.	same
2010	62	42	397	same	8.-10.Sept.	same
2011	64	42	393	same	7.-9. Sept.	same
2012	57	37	400	same	12.-14.Sept.	same
2013	83	45	403	same	11.-13.Sept.	Prague
2014	84	40	413	same	10.-12.Sept.	Poděbrady
2015	113	58	519.	same	9..-11.Sept.	same
2016	94	41	463	same	7.-9.Sept.	same
2017	93	45	480 (est.)	same	6.-8.Sept.	same
	1300	807	8649	TOTAL		

Fig. 10: 25 IDIMT Conferences : 1993 - 2017

2 25 year of IDIMT - A History of Continuity and Change

It is hard to believe that we are celebrating the 25th anniversary of IDIMT. The chronology below shows the remarkable and successful growth of IDIMT over the years. For each year of the IDIMT conference we identify:

- the reference to the proceedings (preceded by "☞")

- a few noteworthy characteristics (identified by "≪ ... ≫") and

- the key topics of the year (identified by " ✎ ").

2.1 KUBOVA HUT', 1993-1994

Fig. 11: Hotel Arnika, Kubova Hut, 1993

1993, The First Conference : ☞ [CD93]
≪ *The first meeting was characterized initial contacts and by a strive for "bilateral balance"* ≫

✎ *Key conference topics: The topics were information management in the classical sense and software engineering in relation to technology and its management. Transition between management systems was a big topic*

Petr Doucek found a reasonable conference site: Hotel Arnika in Kubova Hut', near Vimperk, in the Šumava (Bohemian Woods) some 110 km north of Linz (fig. 11).

The conference facilities were not too good. We had to transport all conference equipment to this location, but it was cosy and since there was no other diversion, we had long discussions at the bar and thus got to know each other really well. In this first meeting we took upon us the challenge of bridging the multidimensional gaps between Linz and Prague.

We were very concerned about a fair balance of really everything in the meeting: the number of papers from both sides, the number of chairpersons, the mix of nationality within sessions, the sequence of speakers, etc. etc. and - I may say - we were successful! Despite the small number of attendees (14) we not only enjoyed the interdisciplinary exchange of ideas, we also recognized the need and potential for further and more intensive communication.

Fig. 11: Vimperk near Kubova Hut'

We quote from the opening paper by Profs. Ehleman and Vodáček: *"...managerial thinking and management systems have been rapidly undergoing substantial, sometimes even painful changes. The political transition [and] the transformation to the market type economy have created quite new tasks and problems we were not used to."*

The 13 presented papers with a total of 151 pages were published as the first volume of the IDIMT-proceedings (fig. 12), see also section 4.

Fig. 12: IDIMT 1993 - cover   Fig. 13: Proceedings of IDIMT 1993

Fig. 14: Jan Ehleman, Jan Skrbek

IDIMT 1994: ☞ [CD94]

≪ *The proceedings were published by the Austrian Computer Society (OCG). The communication location was the bar of the hotel: so we managed to consume all their alcoholic beverages!* ≫

✎ *Key conference topics: 'Transition' in many fields was the overriding theme, especially with respect to the changes in the Czech economy.*

The conviction that the conferences will become a permanent institution, made us think of an appropriate acronym: Petr Doucek coined "Interdisciplinary Information Management Talks (IDIMT)". This expressed most of our intentions : to be *interdisciplinary*, to put *information* at the center of our interest and to use a considerable part of the meetings for *interdisciplinary* and informal *discussions* and not for just presenting papers.

The publication of the proceedings of IDIMT 1994 was handed over to a professional publisher: Oldenbourg Publishers as part of the Publication Series of the Austrian Computer Society (see at left).

Fig. 15: IDIMT 1994

2.2   ZADOV, 1995- 2002

Fig. 16: Hotel Olympia, Zadov

IDIMT 1995: ☞ [CD95]

≪ *Move to Hotel Olympia in Zadov with excellent gastronomy* ≫

✎ *Key conference topics: Issues of networking in office work had their first impact on the programme ("Workgroup computing").*

We had to abandon Kubova Hut' because the hotel was being refurbished. Petr Doucek, after considerable effort and travel selected Hotel Olympia in Zadov. Hotel Olympia was remarkable since it was located in the well known skiing resort of Churanov Mountain. The summit of Churanov (1140 meter) was only a 10-minute walk away from the hotel and the hotel was surrounded by deep, beautiful woods.

Fig. 17: Meetingroom in hotel Olympia, Zadov, 2002

We had a problem finding the hotel driving from Linz. We arrived easily in the right area, but it was already dark and raining, nobody was there to ask and there were no street signs - I actually drove all around Churanov before finally finding the hotel, arriving more than an hour late. Hotel Olympia had much better facilities and especially a very pleasant, comfortable conference room (fig. 17). On the gastronomic side, too, the quality had improved.

1995 was the first truly international meeting with participants from 4 different nations (Austria, Czech Republic, Germany, Poland).

In that year a new format for the proceedings was chosen by our publisher, Oldenbourg, giving the proceedings a much more professional look.

Fig. 18: IDIMT 1995 Proceedings

IDIMT 1996: ☞ [CD96]

≪ *Computer Supported Cooperative Work (CSCW) becomes a strong focus* ≫

✎ *Key conference topics: Tele-training, communication, and technology transfer parallel to transition problems; information management became a standard topic in all following meetings.*

Hotel Olympia in Zadov also proved to us the dynamics inherent in the Czech economy in those days. Year after year there was continuous improvement, something new, something more professional. Mr. Pavlik, the owner, always had a few pleasant surprises for us (fig. 19). The welcome dinner on Wednesday night was always an enjoyable get-together (fig. 33).

Fig. 19: Lunch at Hotel Olympia, Zadov 2001: Petr Doucek, Antonín Rosický, Karel Pstružina

IDIMT 1997: ☞ [HD97]

≪ *Manfred Beneder becomes Co-Editor* ≫

✎ *Key conference topics: Human aspects and issues of systemic thinking appeared, as well as quality management.*

For the first time the conference included two invited speakers: Prof. Franz Pichler from the Kepler University Linz ("On the Concept of Holarchy by Arthur Köstler") and Prof. Jaroslav Vlček ("The Role of Systems Thinking and Systems Methodologies in the actual State of Conditions"). The (pleasant) problem of receiving too many good papers forced us to adopt a new conference scheme: each session is now started with a keynoter introducing a subject, followed by shorter presentations supporting (or opposing) the introduced subject. This new structure has proven to be very helpful until today, providing us with more valuable discussion time than before.

IDIMT 1998: ☞ [HB98]

≪ *We selected Trauner Publishers, Linz as our new publisher. Manfred Beneder and Susanne Hofer become the new editors of the proceedings.* ≫

✎ *Key conference topics: Systemic thinking, quality management, and human interfaces have become central topics. Anticipating future technological advances has become part of the topics we discussed.*

Fig. 20: IDIMT 1998

Due to a change in the publishing arrangements of the Austrian Computer Society, the OCG, we decided to change to a different publisher: the Trauner Verlag Linz (see at left). For this purpose I established a new Publication Series "Informatik" at the Trauner Verlag, Linz. Proceedings of other conferences had also been published in this Series. Today (2012) a total of 38 volumes have appeared in this Series.

Manfred Beneder and Susanne Hofer (fig. 21 and fig. 22) officially became the editors of the IDIMT 1998 proceedings, after having helped to organize the scientific programme of the IDIMT Conferences from the start. The university assistants took over the task of chairing the sessions - an excellent training ground for their involvement in conferences.

Fig. 21: Manfred Beneder

Fig. 22: Susanne Hofer

IDIMT 1999: ☞ [HB99]

≪ *System Sciences (introduced by Matjaž Mulej) becomes a new subject, the conference date is changed to the middle of September in order to fit into university vacation schedules.* ≫

✎ *Key conference topics: Development and Management of IS/IT processes, Cooperative Processes and Human factors.*

Triggered by the keynotes of 1998, systems related papers achieved a prominent place in the programme, especially due to the involvement of Matjaž Mulej (fig. 28).

Fig. 23: Matjaž Mulej

The topic of cooperative environments was especially supported by Konrad Klöckner (fig. 24) and Tom Gross (fig. 25).
Until 1998 the IDIMT conferences had traditionally been held early/middle of October. In 1999 we decided to move to late middle/late September to make attendance easier for our university participants.

Fig. 24: Erwin Grosspietsch, Konrad   Fig. 25: Tom Gross, Christian Hofer, 2002
Klöckner

An effort was also made to give the proceedings a personal touch. Janie Chroust offered to draw a sketch of České Budějovice to head the welcome page. This has also become a tradition.

IDIMT 2000: ☞ [HB00]
≪ holding a Dinner-Talk, e-mail submission becomes standard ≫

✎ Key conference topics: The development of information systems (10 papers out of 32) and human factors (8 papers out of 32), including ethics and regulations became /main subjects of the programme.

We had an official dinner talk (Gerhard Chroust "Internationalization is more than translation!") on Wednesday evening, before the official opening of IDIMT on Thursday morning. A panel discussed the questions of 'Ethics, Regulations and Professionalism' exploring several controversial issues.

In their introduction the editors (Susanne Hofer and Manfred Beneder) stressed the importance and usefulness of e-mail and internet for submitting, reviewing and collecting the papers, not a standard feature in 2000!

IDIMT 2001: ☞ [HC01]

≪ *We have "two prominent Christians" in the team: Christian W. Loesch (reporting on Technology), and Christian Hofer (the new Co-Editor)* ≫

✎ *Key conference topics: Electronic commerce (together with tele-learning, teleteaching, tele-work) and a concern for the SME's, the small and medium enterprises, entered the programme*

A new traditions was established: from this date on Christian Loesch gave a technology forecast every year on certain ICT-technologies and developments (fig. 26). In 2001 he spoke about "'Trends in Business, Technology, and Research & Development". His presentations have become one of the highlights of each of the following IDIMT conferences, see also [Loe12] and [LC17], see also fig. 85.

Fig. 26: Christian Loesch presenting technological forecasts

Manfred Beneder and Susanne Hofer left the Kepler University Linz. Manfred Beneder accepted an interesting and challenging job with a software company, while Susanne Hofer became mother of little Alexander and stayed home for some time.

Christian Hofer (fig. 27), Susanne's husband, took Susanne's place at the institute and also in the organization and the co-editorship of the proceedings - it was a very smooth transition without any problems.

Fig. 27: Christian Hofer

The organizers even remembered that Gerhard Chroust had turned 60 in 2001 and they arranged a very nice celebration (fig. 28 and fig. 29).

Fig. 28: Celebrating Gerhard's 60th birth-day at IDIMT2001: Gerhard Chroust, Mat-jaž Mulej, Petr Doucek

Fig. 29: Janie Chroust, Gerhard Chroust, Petr Doucek

IDIMT 2002: ☞ [HC02]

≪ 10th Anniversary of IDIMT, a Painting Exhibition, a first PhD-day ≫

✎ *Key conference topics: E-commerce and e-Government and associated security problems are important topics. Interdependence and Ethics elicit several papers with a long-range vision. Three papers explicitly address small and medium enterprises.*

We were proud to celebrate the 10th Anniversary of the IDIMT-Conferences. A special cultural event, an exhibition of paintings by Mag. Dr. Traude Loesch ("Impressions of Vienna") and Janie Chroust ("Impressions of Linz") showing views of these two cities, highlighted this event (fig. 31).

Fig. 30: Happy Birthday IDIMT!

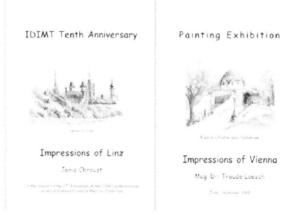

Fig. 31: Painting Exhibition at IDIMT 2002: Traude Loesch and Janie Chroust

Fig. 32: Traude Lösch and Janie Chroust with their pictures

Fig. 33: IDIMT 2002: Welcome party: Erwin Grosspietsch, Lea Nedomová, Gerhard Chroust, Antonín Rosický, Jan Ehleman

Fig. 34: PhD-Day 2002 in Prague

In 2002 we introduced another first: the 'PhD-Student Forum'. Nine students from Austria, the Czech Republic and the Slovak Republic (see left) met in Prague one day before the IDIMT Conference und the auspices of former rector associate professor Jaroslava Durákováá. She invited all participants to a private audience and to the cultural part of the PhD-day. The students discussed their specific PhD-themes and also issues of general relevance of their studies both in a formal meeting and in informal discussions. The meeting was moderated by Antonin Lavrin. Besides the technical-scientific discussions we also organized a tour of Prague including the famous Charles University in Prague, the oldest University in the Middle Europe. When joining the IDIMT Conference in Zadov on the following day, they presented their ideas and findings.

This PhD-day triggered further actions, including further invitations of Czech and Slovak PhD students to meetings. We organized one of these common actions in May 2003 in co-operation with the TU in Kosice [KG03]. We split it into three sessions with the following session leaders as invited speakers:
Prof. Anton Lavrin (Slovak Republic),
Prof. Karel Pstružina (Czech Republic)
Dr. Antonín Rosický (Czech Republic).
Also professor Richard Hindls - the dean of the faculty - with his vice dean for research and development work, professor Stanislava Hronová, also took part as a guest of honor at this conference. In 2006 [Chr06a, DHCK06, Chr06b] and 2007 we repeated the idea of the PhD-day very successfully by discussing both the value of a PhD-degree and the procedures in different countries in order to become a PhD.

2.3 ČESKÉ BUDĚJOVICE, 2003- 2007

Fig. 35: The central square of České Budějovice

IDIMT 2003: ☞ [CH03]

≪ We moved IDIMT to České Budějovice ≫

✎ Key conference topics: 'Trends' is a favorite topic in the papers, followed by system thinking, e-business, cooperative environments.

Fig. 36: České Bu-
dějovice

In Spring of 2003 we received a very unpleasant message: due to a misunderstanding the Hotel Olympia in Zadov was unable to accommodate our group, not even if we adjusted our confe-rence dates slightly. A hectic search began for a replacement. Thanks to Prof. Helmut Renöckl (Kepler University Linz and Uni-versity of Southern Bohemia) and his assistant Martin Bilek, we were able to find a new location: the "Hotel Garni p.v.t." (fig. 37), in the historical city,České Budějovice. The city was founded in 1265 by the famous King Přemysl Otak and always played a key role in the Čzech Republic. It has preserved a beautiful and im-pressive market place and also many small,picturesque streets (see fig. 35).

It is world-famous for its beer. In the 19th century České Budě-
jovice was also famous as being one of the end station of the Horse Railway from Linz to Southern Bohemia, the first public railway in continental Europe, see section 9.

Fig. 37: Hotel garni p.v.t., České Budějovice

Lunch and dinner were arranged in the Restaurant Metropol se-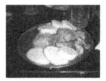veral steps away from the hotel. This offered the possibility of getting to know Czech cuisine more thoroughly and appreciating the famous roast pork.

Honoring České Budějovice's long standing brewing tradition, we visited the famous Brewery in Budějovice as part of the official conference programme.

Fig. 38: Delicious roast pork

Fig. 39: Lunch at restaurant Metropol - Petr Doucek, Karel Pstružina

IDIMT 2004: [HC04]

≪ *The conference proceedings received a new cover layout* ≫

✎ *Key conference topics: e-society, educational aspects, cooperative environments and economic aspects.*

In this year we were able to welcome the Czech Republic as a member of the European Union: the opening address was "Welcome to IDIMT! Welcome to Europe!" We also observed that information and its management is a key concern of the European Union and its research programs. IDIMT has proved itself to be a worthy contributor to the common European goal.

The effects of electronic communication on all aspects of society have become an important topic. The effects on teaching and learning also received special attention.

In 2004 our publisher, Trauner Verlag, decided to reorganize he appearance of all their published publications. The proceedings of IDIMT were given a new cover layout (see at right), a considerable improvement to its appearance.

Fig. 40: IDIMT 2004, a new cover

IDIMT 2005: ☞ [HC05]

≪ *Christoph Hoyer becomes Co-Editor* ≫

✎ *Key conference topics: European Projects and SMEs, Innovation and Creative Thinking, Cooperative Information Environments, and Human Factors.*

Christoph Hoyer, who succeeded Christian Hofer at the Kepler University Linz, took over the co-editorship of the proceedings. Again the transition took place without any problems.

In order to accommodate more papers and discussions we started the conference with an opening session on Wednesday in the late afternoon. Topics of societal implications gained more impact in the submitted papers.

Fig. 41: Christoph Hoyer

IDIMT 2006: ☞ [Dou06]

≪ *Another PhD-day was organized in* ≫

✎ *Key conference topics: Innovation and New Technologies are leading topics, 5 papers discuss European issues of research and especially education, software project management makes an entry into the list of topics*

We revived the idea of a PhD-day, and with the help of Christoph Hoyer we organized this event on the day before the conference (fig. 43). As a topic we chose "The Impact and Value of a PhD in the Information Society". Moderated by Gerhard Chroust and Petr Doucek eight students from 5 countries (Austria, Czech Republic, Germany, Hungary, and Pakistan) discussed for a full day procedures, curricula and the resulting appreciation of a PhD-degree in the various countries. Certain interesting details and differences came up in these discussions. The findings were later collected in a small proceedings booklet [Dou06]. A guided tour of České Budějovice including the magnificent City Hall gave us an impression of the past of this city.

Fig. 42: PhD-day 2006

Fig. 43: Shahid Nazir Bhatti (Pakistan) and Christoph Hoyer

Fig. 44: IDIMT 2006

Fig. 45: Dinner in České Budějovice, Maria Raffai and Christian Loesch

Fig. 46: Dinner inČeské Budějovice, Traude Loesch and Gerhard Chroust

Fig. 47: Dinner in České Budějovice

IDIMT 2006 was an ideal platform for presenting the results of scientific work by young and/or younger colleagues and PhD students. We again added a PhD-day with a session during the main conference [Chr06a, DHCK06, Chr06b].

Fig. 48: IDIMT 2006: Petr Doucek

IDIMT 2007: ☞ [HCD07]

≪ *We celebrated 15 Years of IDIMT, and organized another PhD-day in České Budějovice* ≫

✎ *Key conference topics: System theories occupies a large portion of the programm together with European projects, especially personal experiences with them. Four papers give an overview of the history of IDIMT.*

IDIMT 2007 was the 15th IDIMT conference in succession and we decided to celebrate this significantly. As a preparation of IDIMT 2007 we sent explicit invitations to participants from previous IDIMT-conferences asking them to attend,

The success of the 2006 PhD-day had encouraged us to repeat it in 2007. In 2007 we challenged our PhD-students to conceptualize a EU-project to which all students should be able to contribute. To enable a better assessment of the implications of projects in cooperation with the European Union we asked Mag. Edith Mayer, one of the experts of the CATT Innovation Management GmbH in Linz to hold a presentation on approaches, chances and problems of European Projects.

A bus tour to visit beautiful Ceský Krumlow together with a lively celebration dinner honored the 15th anniversary of the IDIMT conferences. From then on bus tours to hold the conference banquet in a neighboring, culturally interesting location became the rule.

2007 proved to be an ideal platform for presenting the results of scientific work by young and/or younger colleagues and PhD students.

Fig. 49: Visiting Ceský Krumlow

Fig. 50: Celebrating 15 years of IDIMT in
Ceský Krumlow

Fig. 51: Celebrating 15 years of IDIMT in
Ceský Krumlow

Fig. 52: Discussion with PhD-students at IDIMT 2007

Fig. 53: IDIMT 2007: conference break (A. Rosický, A. Lavrin, J. Klas)

2.4   JINDŘICHŮV HRADEC, 2008 - 2012

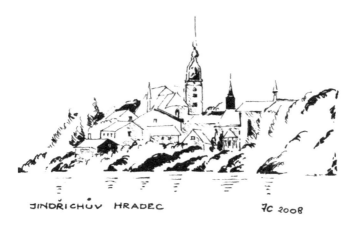

Fig. 54: Jindřichův Hradec

IDIMT 2008: ☞ [CDK08]

≪ *Move to Jindřichův Hradec, Jan KLAS becomes Co-Editor, another PhD-day* ≫

✎ *Key conference topics: Questions of project management (performance, information management, human factors) gain more prominence. Security and Safety are a key concern. Systems thinking is oriented to project management*

This year brought a change of location. The major reason for this was that the capacity of the hotel in České Budějovice had become too small for the growing number of participants of IDIMT - a very pleasing reason. Jindřichův Hradec turned out to be a picturesque historical town, beautifully situated on a lake, with a very impressive castle, a prominent church, an a architecturally interesting market place. We stayed in the Grand Hotel on the Main Square.

We took over the successful PhD-day concept from the previous year: a dozen young PhD-students met one day before the actual conference in order to tackle a truly European challenge: discussion of advantages and disadvantages of studying abroad during or immediately adjacent to one's PhD-studies or later on. They discovered that the conditions for studying, funding and subsidies are considerably different in the various countries.

Fig. 55: Demonstration of knights fighting

Fig. 56: Jan Klas

Jan KLAS took over the editorship of the proceedings from Christoph Hoyer, and also the organisation of the IDIMT conference with all kinds of "small" but essential problems (see at left). This was not easy because much of the know-how about the proceedings and the organisation had up to now been located in Linz and passed on from one assistant to the next. From now on everything had to be arranged in Prague. The logistic computer support had to be newly set up in Prague - the printing, however, was still done in Linz, due to the good cooperation between the Copy Service of the Johannes Kepler University and Trauner publishers. Jan had to keep up with a growing number of papers.

IDIMT 2009: ☞ [DCO09]

≪ *Václav Oškrdal takes over the Co-Editorship, Antonín Pavlíček takes on the organisation of the IDIMT conference* ≫

✏ *Key conference topics: Human and social issues gain prominence when considering software intensive systems, Computer Support Cooperative Work (CSCW) having held its prominent place since 1995.*

Fig. 57: Václav Oškrdal   *Fig. 58: Antonín Pavlíček*

We had a change in the organisation of IDIMT and the proceedings: Václav Oškrdal took on this responsible and difficult task. A new scientific achievement for IDIMT was the inclusion of the proceedings in the American scientific database Web of Science (CPCI-S - Conference Proceeding Citation Index- Science) operated by Thomson Reuters [Tho12]. This results in all IDIMT proceedings dating from 2004 on being included in this world-known scientific database. The indexing also implies among other advantages that contributions presented at the IDIMT conferences are accepted by the Ministry of Education, Youth and Sports of the Czech Republic as an output of research and development work. An additional advantage were the statistics Thomas Reuters provided, see also section 4.5.

Fig. 59: Jindřichův Hradec

Our bus tour took us to one of the most remarkable cities in the area: Slavonice (fig. 61, fig. 62). It is located to the south-east of Jindřichův Hradec within a few kilometers away from the Austrian border.

Fig. 60: Discussing "The Magic of 'Open Everything'": M. Sonntag, A. Pavlíček, V. Oš-krdal, C. W. Loesch

Fig. 61: IDIMT 2009 : visit to Slavonice

Fig. 62: Slavonice, Sgrafitti-house

IDIMT 2010: ☞ [DCO10]

≪ We move the conference to Hotel Concertino ≫

✎ Key conference topics: Innovation became a key topic, as was Culture and Ethics, discussed with respect to globalization and internationality.

Fig. 63: Grand Hotel, Jindrichuv Hradec

We decided to change the hotel: we moved to the Hotel Concertino, just on the other side of the Main Square, opposite the Grand Hotel. It offered a good meeting-room facility and an improvement of room quality.

We visited Červena Lhotá, the "red" castle romantically located on an artificial lake.

We had a peasant-style conference dinner in a picturesque restaurant (fig. 66).

Fig. 64: Jindřichův Hradec

Fig. 65: Červena Lhotá

Fig. 66: IDIMT 2010: Walking to the conference dinner

IDIMT 2011: ☞ [DCO11]

≪ *Introduction of a Posters Session* ≫

✎ *Key conference topics: complex systems, interdisciplinary, regional emergencies,*

Human resources, human well-being, socio-economics

Human aspects are now a prominent feature emphasizing human well-being, including social computing, privacy, and socio-economic considerations. Systemic reaction to regional disaster gains prominence.

The IDIMT conferences have become more attractive and thus we received more papers. In order to accommodate the increased influx of papers and to give younger scientists a chance of publication, we have accepted four posters which have been presented briefly during the conference - another chance for young scientists.

Fig. 67: Jindřichův Hra-

Fig. 68: Discussion after the session

Fig. 69: Konrad Klöckner,   Hotel Concertino,   Erwin Schoitsch

IDIMT 2012: : ☞ [DCO12]

≪ *20 year celebration, we publish a special historical book [CD12]* ≫

✎ *Key conference topics: Human aspects are still a prominent feature, including social computing and business considerations, A new topic is introduced 'systems of systems', their impact and their reliability, economic issues and ICT, and social responsibility, and - obviously - a historical retrospective*

The 20th IDIMT Conference kept to its regular scientific programm [DCO12] but in addition we took a look back over the last 20 years. We published a special booklet, containing retrospective views of the IDIMT conferences and also the collection of all technical reports given by Christian Loesch since 2000 [CD12]. This tradition was repeated for the 25-year celebration by two books, one telling the story of all IDIMT conferences (this book) [CDN17] and the second one containing all 18 lectures (2000 -2017) by Christian Loesch [LC17], see section 3.

Fig. 70: 20 Years of IDIMT

Fig. 71: Dinner buffet at Hotel Concertino

Fig. 72: Dinner at IDIMT 2012

We held our celebration dinner in Telč, another lovely Bohemian city.

Fig. 73: Participants of IDIMT 2012, Telč

2.5   PRAHA, 2013

Fig. 74: Prague, Charles Bridge

IDIMT 2013: ☞ [DCO13]

≪ We moved to Praha, parallel to the CONFENIS 2013 conference, allowing switching between both conferences, paper submission by Easy Chair system ≫

✎ Key conference topics: social media, innovation, corporate performance

In 2013 we joined forces with the CONFENIS 2013 conference in a joint and parallel conference in Prague. We achieved some synergetic effects by listening to several lectures of the parallel conference. And we all had enough time to enjoy fascinating Prague, including a boat trip on the Moldawa. For the first time we also used the conference administration system EasyChair for paper submission.

Fig. 75: Jan Skrbek on 'warning cars'

Fig. 76: Confenis-2013, Prague

2.6 PODĚBRADY, 2014 - ?

Fig. 77: Poděbrady, the castle seen from the river Janie Chroust 2014

IDIMT 2014: ☞ [DCO14]

≪ *We moved to Poděbrady. Hotel and conference site are separate, but it proved to be a very cosy location* ≫

✎ *Key conference topics: disaster management, social media, Wisdom of crowds, Cloud computing*

Fig. 78: Poděbrady: Statue of George Poděbrad (1420-1471)

Fig. 79: Poděbrady: Fountain and Park

In 2014 we returned to a smaller, quieter place, to Poděbrady, a traditional and typical spa-center and an old historical town, founded in the 13th century being of considerable political importance during the 14th to 16th century, especially during the reign of Georg von Poděbrad (1420 - 1471).

IDIMT 2015: ☞ [DCO15]

≪ *surprisingly high number of accepted papers, 2 streams of presentations, biggest proceedings ever* ≫

✎ *Key conference topics: resilience, academic and business cooperation, social media, e-sourcing and e-procurement, Ethics, health-data*

2015 brought a pleasant but inconvenient surprise. We received too many good papers to accommodate them in our classical organisation: 58 papers with 113 co-authors yielding an all-time record of 519 pages of proceedings. We had to decide straight away to run the conference in two parallel streams. This decision was made easier due to the fact that in the course of the last years we had observed a strong trend from technological/managerial topics to much 'softer' topics, such as the impacts of ICT on society and humans plus their consequences. To some extent this was also reflected in the two streams. We also enjoyed the park (see below).

Fig. 80: R. Delina on 'E-Procurement'

Fig. 81: The colonnada in Poděbrady

IDIMT 2016: ☞ [DCO16]

≪ *We are able to handle to increased number of papers; the migration crisis of 2015 is reflected in the presentations* ≫

✎ *Key conference topics: Digital Economy, Digital Markets, Innovation, Crisis Management, E-Health, Cyber-Security, Smart Systems*

2016 was year where also many very good contributions appeared in the conference. Traditionally most quality papers were in the sessions of "Social Media and Information management", "Corporate and ICT Management" and "The Multiply Roles of the Public in Crisis Management". Surprisingly there was a relative small of quality contributions and as a consequence of attendance the session "Cyber Security", which became a very hot topic in 2017.

Fig. 82: M. Sonntag on 'Cyber Security'

IDIMT 2017: ☞ [DCO17]

≪ *25 year celebration, 2 additional books published [CDN17, LC17]* ≫

✎ *Key conference topics: Social Media, ICT support for Health Management, Crisis Management, 25 years of IDIMT*

This year (2017), we celebrated our 25th anniversary in Poděbrady. In the opening sessions we gave a short overview of the history of IDIMT, both with respect to the contents and form, but also mentioning the 6 different locations of the conference. For this purpose we published two additional books: one containing the detailed history of the IDIMT conferences adding pictures documenting our long and very successful history [CDN17]. A visit to the impressive Škoda factory in Mláda Boleslav showed the effectiveness of ICT in the world of production and a second book containing all (now 18) lectures held by Christian Loesch, [LC17].

Fig. 83: Škoda-Museum in Mláda Boleslav

Fig. 84: End of teh conference : Erwin and Elfi Schoitsch

3   Memorial publications: 25 Years of IDIMT Conferences

25 years of continuous yearly conferences it worth a look back. We have come a long way from the first IDIMT conference in 1993 to 2017 in Poděbrady. The size of the conference, its impact and the participants have changed. In order to celebrate this achievement and to keep some of the memories alive, two books were published separately and are now available in the international book market. One book (this ones) captures some of the details of this impressive history of the conferences in total, including key acting persons. Also, one highlight since 2000 were the introductory lectures by Christian Loesch, presenting a view of the technologicall/economic situation of the ICT-industry. These 18 lectures were also published in separate book [LC17].

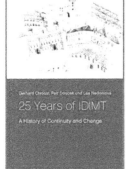

25year IDIMT Conferences (1993 – 2017)

Memorial Publications

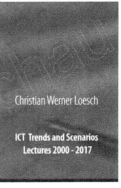

Books on Demand, Norderstedt, Germany, 2017

60 pages	244 pages,
hard-copy 14 €, e-book 4,50 €	hard-copy 15 €. e-book 8 €
ISBN 978-3-74480-9573	ISBN 978-3-74489-4265

Order information:
BoD Buchshop https://www.bod.de/buchshop/
and in international bookshops like Amazon.

Fig. 85: Two Memorial Publications celebrating 25 years of IDIMT

4   The proceedings of the IDIMT Conferences

One of the visible outcomes of the IDIMT Conferences are the proceedings: they are proud record of our work (see below). The impressive collection of the first 15 volumes is shown in fig. 92. It also shows the changing layout of the proceedings. For the time being the design of the 2006-conference will still be used in the future (fig. 93). Over the years more than 800 (co-)authors have contributed more than 600 papers on almost 7000 pages. On average we printed approximately 150 copies of each volume. From 2004 onward the proceedings are also available on IDIMT's homepage (www.idimt.org).

4.1   The growth of the proceedings

Parallel to the growth of the Conference the size of the proceedings have also grown from a mere 150 to almost 500 pages, see fig. 86 and fig. 87.

year	au-thors	Pa-pers	pages	Conference chairs and editors	Date of Conference	Location
1993	14	13	151	Gerhard Chroust, Petr Doucek	6.-8.Oct.	Kubova Huť
1994	27	23	233	same	9. -11.Nov.	same
1995	33	25	228	same	8.-10.Oct.	Zadov
1996	30	21	215	same	16.-18.Oct.	same
1997	35	30	320	Susanne Hofer, Petr Doucek	15.-17.Oct.	same
1998	39	27	390	Susanne Hofer, Manfred Beneder	21.-23.Oct.	same
1999	46	34	424	same	02.-03.Sept.	same
2000	48	32	440	same	20.-22.Sept.	same
2001	45	29	397	Christian Hofer, Gerhard Chroust	19.-21.Sept.	same
2002	38	24	350	same	11.-13.Sept.	same
2003	38	24	310	same	10.-12.Sept.	České Budějovice
2004	31	23	304	same	15.-17.Sept.	same
2005	30	22	313	Christian Hoyer, Gerhard Chroust	14.-16.Sept.	same
2006	45	29	364	same	13.-15.Sept.	same
2007	38	27	383	Christoph Hoyer, Gerhard Chroust, Petr Doucek	12.-14.Sept.	same
2008	53	33	455	Gerhard Chroust, Petr Doucek, Jan Kias	10.-12.Sept.	Jindřichův Hradec
2009	61	42	423	Petr Doucek, Gerhard Chroust, Vaclav Oškrdal	9.-11.Sept.	same
2010	62	42	397	same	8.-10.Sept.	same
2011	64	42	393	same	7.-9.Sept.	same
2012	57	37	400	same	12.-14.Sept.	same
2013	83	45	403	same	11.-13.Sept.	Prague
2014	84	40	413	same	10.-12.Sept.	Poděbrady
2015	113	58	519	same	9.-11.Sept.	same
2016	94	41	463	same	7.-9.Sept.	same
2017	93	45	456	same	6.-8.Sept.	same
	1300	807	8625	TOTAL		

Fig. 86: IDIMT Conferences 1993 - 2017

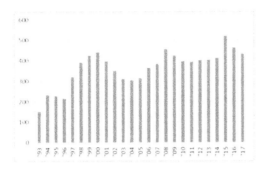

Fig. 87: Growth of pages of the Proceedings (1993 - 2017)

4.2   Editors

The production of proceedings is a difficult, often frustrating and time-consuming job, often not adequately recognized. The editor(s) have to encourage the authors to submit their final papers in time, conforming to the prescribed form with respect to size, layout and type font. These papers have to be aggregated, the cover and the table of contents created and finally handed over to the printer. Since 2013 we use the EasyChair paper-submission tool.

The editors of the proceedings deserve a special thank-you from all participants and from the scientific community in general.

Over the years many persons have acted as editors, resp. co-editors:

- Manfred Beneder (1998 - 2000)

- Gerhard Chroust (1993 - 1996, 2001 - 2017)

- Petr Doucek (1993 - 1997, 2008 - 2017)

- Christian Hofer (2001 - 2004)

- Susanne Hofer (1997 - 2000)

- Christoph Hoyer (2005 - 2007)

- Jan Klas (2008)

- Václav Oškrdal (2009 - 2017)

Manfred Beneder Gerhard Chroust Petr Doucek   Christian Hofer Susanne Hofer

Christoph Hoyer   Jan Klas   Lea Nedomová Václav Oškrdal   Antonín
                                                                  Pavlíček

Fig. 88: Editors and organizers of the IDIMT conference

4.3   Authors of conference contributions

The key to a successful conference and (thus to good proceedings) are the authors. The growth of the number of authors and papers is shown in fig. 89. The most active authors in the time frame from 2011-2017 are shown in fig. 90. It is also interesting to see the distribution over different nations in fig. 91.

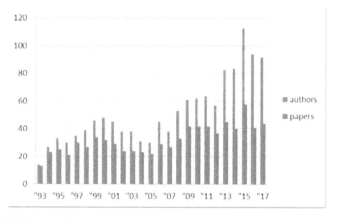

Fig. 89: Number of authors and papers of the IDIMT Conferences 1993 - 2017

DOUCEK P	24	ROSICKY A	8	SEMERADOVA T	5
MULEJ M	22	SCHOITSCH E	8	TKAC M	5
FISCHER I	16	SUDZINA F	8	WAGNER I	5
CHROUST G	15	CAPEK J	7	ZELKO M	5
PAVLICEK A	14	HOLA I	7	AUMAYR G	4
SONNTAG M	13	PUCIHAR A	7	FIALA T	4
CANCER V	11	BASL J	6	HANCLOVA J	4
DELINA R	11	KUBAT D	6	HELFERT M	4
MINISTR J	11	LAVRIN A	6	HRAST A	4
SIGMUND T	11	LENART G	6	IANDOS I	4
SKRBEK J	11	DORCAK P	5	JANKE F	4
LOESCH CW	10	GALA T	5	KOZEL R	4
MARYSKA M	10	GROSSPIETSCH KE	5	MANDAK J	4
NOVOTNY O	10	KLAS J	5	NEDOMOVA L	4
SVATA V	10	MILDEOVA S	5	POLLAK F	4
GROSS T	9	OSKRDAL V	5	ROSI B	4
KLOCKNER K	9	PETERA P	5	ROZEHNAL P	4
VLTAVSKA K	9	POTOCAN V	5	SILAYEVA IA	4
ANTLOVA K	8	RAFFAI M	5	SMUTNY Z	4
LANGHAMROVA J	8	SAROTAR-ZIZEK S	5	VARGA A	4
NEUHAUER G	8				

Fig. 90: Co-Authors of papers (2011-2016)

CZECH REPUBLIC	236	LUXEMBOURG	2
AUSTRIA	56	POLAND	2
SLOVAKIA	37	RUSSIA	2
SLOVENIA	34	TAIWAN	2
GERMANY	28	USA	2
DENMARK	5	BRAZIL	1
HUNGARY	5	FINLAND	1
FRANCE	3	ITALY	1
IRELAND	3	SWITZERLAND	1
BELGIUM	2	THAILAND	1
CANADA	2	UKRAINE	1
CROATIA	2	VIETNAM	1

Fig. 91: Nationality of authors (2011-2016)

4.4   The Front-covers of the Proceedings

Over time the layout of the proceedings has considerably changes (fig 92), partially because of our changes of publisher. They were

Department of Systems Analysis, University of Economics Prague, 1993 :   The proceeding of the 1993 conference were published by Petr Doucek's institute, see fig. 12.

Austrian Computer Society (OCG), 1994-1997 : With the success of the first conference we became more ambitious and published the proceedings under the auspices of the OCG which had a cooperation with Oldenbourg Publishers in Munich.

Trauner Publishers Linz, 1998 - now : For various reasons we then printed our Proceedings at the Trauner Publishers Linz. The proceedings had one style of layout from 1998 -2003, and from 2004 onward a much more elaborate one which we still use (fig. 93).

Fig. 92: IDIMT proceedings 1993 - 2006

Fig. 93: IDIMT 2017 - Cover

4.5   Distribution of subject and topics

The subjects topics of the papers varied y over time as a consequence of the changing needs and interests of the field and of the researchers. The distribution of major areas of publication for the year 2004-2017 are shown in fig. 94. Note that due to different counting methods the numbers, the various statistics are not fully consistent with one another.

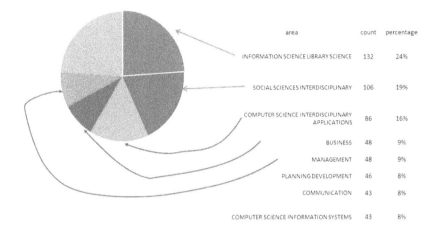

area	count	percentage
INFORMATION SCIENCE LIBRARY SCIENCE	132	24%
SOCIAL SCIENCES INTERDISCIPLINARY	106	19%
COMPUTER SCIENCE INTERDISCIPLINARY APPLICATIONS	86	16%
BUSINESS	48	9%
MANAGEMENT	48	9%
PLANNING DEVELOPMENT	46	8%
COMMUNICATION	43	8%
COMPUTER SCIENCE INFORMATION SYSTEMS	43	8%

Fig. 94: Distribution of topic areas (2004-2017)

With respect to the key words which where in heavy use, we show the word clouds of 2017, 2012, 2007 - and as a contrast those from 1993. One notices the interesting shifts of importance over the years.

Fig. 95: Distribution of words in the titles of papers (2017)

Fig. 96: Distribution of words in the titles of papers (2012)

Fig. 97: Distribution of words in the titles of papers (2007)

Fig. 98: Distribution of words in the titles of papers (1993)

5   Words of Thanks

The preparation and realization of IDIMT 2017 would not have been possible without the support of diverse organizations and persons. Therefore we would like to thank the following for providing the organizational infrastructure.:

- the University of Economics Prague for the project IGA 409017,

- the Faculty of Informatics and Statistics of University of Economics, Prague, and

- the Johannes Kepler University Linz.

Our further thanks go to:

- Petr Doucek for chairing the Organizing Committee, for arranging the conference location, the hotels and the greatly appreciated evening event,

- Lea Nedomová, for co-chairing the Organizing Committee and for her support in performing the necessary administrative tasks,

- Lea Nedomová and Antonín Pavlíček for organizing the program, the reviews, keeping contact with all involved speakers, reminding the authors,

- Václav Oskrdal who is responsible for arranging and assembling the selected papers into the proceedings,

- all Keynote Speakers, speakers and contributors of papers,

- all members of the Programme committee and the Session Chairpersons for soliciting contributors and creating an interesting and compact programme,

- all reviewers providing critical remarks for improving the papers,

- the Trauner Verlag for acting as the publisher of our conference, and

- all other unnamed persons contributing to the success of this conference.

We want to thank all our session chairs, session organizers, speakers and reviewers and especially the Organizers and Editors of the IDIMT Conferences.

We would like to extend our thanks to the publication team of the OCG and then to the publication team of Trauner Verlag Linz, our current publisher, and its editorial staff, especially Mrs. Mag. Elisabeth Kindermann and Ms. Noemi Tifan for support and helpful advice.

THANK YOU!

6   Literature

[BJNM13]   J. Basl, P. Jasek, O. Novotny, and Tjoa A M., editors. *CONFENIS-2013, 7th International Conference on Research and Practical Issues of Enterprise Information Systems, Sept 11-13, 2013*. Schriftenreihe Informatik no. 41,Trauner Publ. Linz, 2013, 2013.

[CD93]   G. Chroust and P. Doucek, editors. *Information Management Workshop '93*. Dept. of Systems Analysis, Univ. of Economics, Prag, 1993, 1993.

[CD94]   G. Chroust and P. Doucek, editors. *IDIMT'94 : 2nd Interdisciplinary Information Management Talks*. Schriftenreihe der Österr. Computergesellschaft, no. 74 Oldenbourg, 1994.

[CD95]   G. Chroust and P. Doucek, editors. *IDIMT-95 : 3nd Interdisciplinary Information Management Talks*. Schriftenreihe der Österr. Computergesellschaft, no. 85, Oldenbourg, 1995.

[CD96]   G. Chroust and P. Doucek, editors. *IDIMT-96: Interdisciplinary Information Management Talks 1996*. Schriftenreihe der Österr. Computergesellschaft, Oldenbourg 1996, 1996.

[CD12]   G. Chroust and P. Doucek, editors. *A short History over 20 Years of IDIMT Conferences*. Inst. for Systems Engineering and Automation, J. Kepler University Linz, Austria, Nr SEA-SR-36, Nov. 2012, 2012.

[CDK08]   G. Chroust, P. Doucek, and J. Klas, editors. *IDIMT-2008 - Managing the Unmanageable - 16th Interdisciplinary Information Management Talks*. Verlag Trauner Linz, 2008, 2008.

[CDN17]   G. Chroust, P. Doucek, and L. Nedomová, editors. *25 Years of IDIMT: A History of Continuity and Change*. Books on Demand, Norderstedt, Germany, 2017 (hard copy and e-book), 2017.

[CH03]   G. Chroust and C. Hofer, editors. *IDIMT-2003, 11th Interdisciplinary Information Management Talks, Sept, 2003, Budweis*. Verlag Trauner Linz, 2003, 2003.

[Chr06a]   G. Chroust. Phd-day 2006 at IDIMT - a retrospective. In *PhD-Day 2006 at IDIMT: The final presentation*, pages 41–52. University of Economics, Prague, Fac. of Informatics and Statistics, Scientific and Research Papers, No. 10, Nov. 2006, 2006.

[Chr06b]   G. Chroust. Phd-day 2006 at IDIMT - a retrospective. In *The Impact and Value of a PhD in the Information Society*, pages 53–59. University of Economics, Prague, Fac. of Informatics and Statistics, Scientific and Research Papers, No. 10, Nov. 2006, 2006.

[Chr07]   G. Chroust. 15 years IDIMT - 15 years of change. In G. Chroust, P. Dou-
           cek, and C. Hoyer, editors, *IDIMT-2007 - 15th Interdisciplinary Information
           Management Talks*, pages 119–141. Verlag Trauner Linz, 2007, 2007.

[DCO09]   P. Doucek, G. Chroust, and V. Oskrdal, editors. *IDIMT 2009 - System and
           Humans - A Complex Relationship, Sept. 9-11, 2009*. Trauner Verlag Linz,
           2009, 2009.

[DCO10]   P. Doucek, G. Chroust, and V. Oskrdal, editors. *IDIMT 2010 Information
           Technology - Human Values, Innovation and Economy, Sept 2010*. Trauner
           Verlag Linz, 2010, 2010.

[DCO11]   P. Doucek, G. Chroust, and V. Oskrdal, editors. *IDIMT-2011 Interdiscipli-
           narity in Complex Systems, vol 36, Sept 2011*. Trauner Verlag Linz, 2011,
           2011.

[DCO12]   P. Doucek, G. Chroust, and V. Oskrdal, editors. *IDIMT 2012 ICT-Support for
           Complex Systems, vol.38 Sept 2012*. Trauner Verlag Linz, 2012, 2012.

[DCO13]   P. Doucek, G. Chroust, and V. Oskrdal, editors. *IDIMT-2013 Information
           Technology, Human Values, Innovation and Economy*. Trauner Verlag Linz,
           Sept. 2013, 2013.

[DCO14]   P. Doucek, G. Chroust, and V. Oskrdal, editors. *IDIMT-2014 Networking
           Societies - Cooperation and Conflict*. Trauner Verlag Linz, Sept. 2014, 2014.

[DCO15]   P. Doucek, G. Chroust, and V. Oskrdal, editors. *IDIMT-2015, Information
           Technology and Society - Interaction and Interdependence*. Trauner Verlag
           Linz, Sept. 2015, 2015.

[DCO16]   P. Doucek, G. Chroust, and V. Oskrdal, editors. *IDIMT-2016, Informati-
           on Technology, Society and Economy, Strategic Cross-Influences*. Trauner
           Verlag Linz, Sept. 2016, 2016.

[DCO17]   P. Doucek, G. Chroust, and V. Oskrdal, editors. *IDIMT-2017, Digitalization
           in Management, Society and Economy*. Trauner Verlag Linz, no 46, Sept.
           2017, 2017.

[DHCK06]   P. Doucek, C. Hoyer, G. Chroust, and J. Klas, editors. *The Impact and Value
           of a PhD in the Information Society*. University of Economics, Prague, Fac.
           of Informatics and Statistics, Scientific and Research Papers, No. 10, Nov.
           2006, 2006. Chroust-06j.

[Dou06]   P. Doucek. The history of the idimt conferences. In C. Hoyer and G. Chroust,
           editors, *IDIMT 2006 - 14th Interdisciplinary Information Management Talks*,
           pages 11–16. Verlag Trauner, Linz, 2006, 2006.

[HB98]   S. Hofer and M. Beneder, editors. *IDIMT'98, 6th Interdisciplinary Informati-
           on Management Talks*. Universitätsverlag Rudolf Trauner, Linz 1998, 1998.

[HB99]   S. Hofer and M. Beneder, editors. *IDIMT'99 : 7th Interdisciplinary Information Management Talks*. Trauner Verlag, Linz 1999, 1999.

[HB00]   S. Hofer and M. Beneder, editors. *IDIMT-2000: 8th Interdisciplinary Information Management Talks, Trauner, Linz*, 2000.

[HC01]   C. Hofer and G. Chroust, editors. *IDIMT-2001, 9th Interdisciplinary Information Management Talkstop, Sept, 2001, Zadov*. Verlag Trauner Linz 2001, 2001.

[HC02]   C. Hofer and G. Chroust, editors. *IDIMT-2002, 10th Interdisciplinary Information Management Talks, Sept, 2002, Zadov*. Verlag Trauner Linz, 2002, 2002.

[HC04]   C. Hofer and G. Chroust, editors. *IDIMT 2004 - 12th Interdisciplinary Information Management Talks*. Verlag Trauner Linz,2004, 2004.

[HC05]   C. Hoyer and G. Chroust, editors. *IDIMT 2005 - 13th Interdisciplinary Information Management Talks*. Verlag Trauner, Linz, 2005, 2005.

[HCD07]   C. Hoyer, G. Chroust, and P. Doucek, editors. *IDIMT-2007 - 15th Interdisciplinary Information Management Talks*. Verlag Trauner Linz, 2007, 2007.

[HD97]   S. Hofer and P. Doucek, editors. *IDIMT'97, 5th Interdisciplinary Information Management Talks*. Schriftenreihe der Österreichischen Computergesellschaft, Oldenbourg 1997, 1997.

[KG03]   J. Klas and S. Gregor. *Information Management and Society*. Oeconomica, Praha 2003, 2003.

[LC17]   C.W. Loesch and G. Chroust (ed.). *ICT Trends and Scenarios: Lectures 2000 - 2017*. Books on Demand, Norderstedt, Germany, 2017 (hard copy and e-book), 2017.

[Loe12]   C.W. Loesch. 20 years IDIMT - ICT trends and scenarios reflected in IDIMT conferences. In G. Chroust, P. Doucek, and C.W. Loesch, editors, *20 Years of IDIMT Conferences - Looking Back*. Inst. for Systems Engineering and Automation, J. Kepler University Linz, Austria, Nr SEA-SR-35, Sept. 2012, 2012.

[Tho12]   Thomson Reuters. Web of knowledge [v.5.7] - web of science citation report. http://apps.webofknowledge.com/ cited 3.7.2012, 2012.

7   List of Figures

Abbildungsverzeichnis

8   Glimpses from IDIMT Conferences (1997 - 2017)

This is a random selection, many supplied by Antonín Pavlíček. Find more on Flicker (https://www.flickr.com/photos/136266358@N02/albums/with/72157673023064402).

2017

9   Linz - Southern Bohemia : A Historical Connection

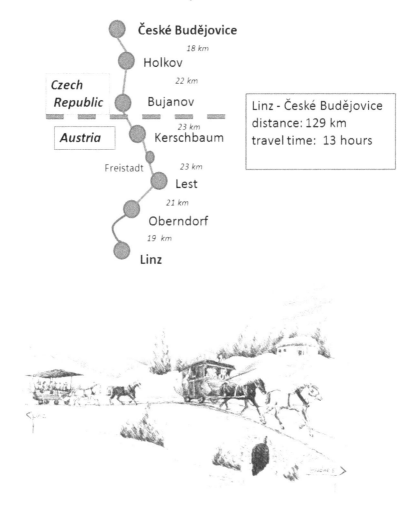

Fig. 99: Travelling from Linz to České Budějovice, anno 1850 (J. Chroust, 2017)

10   Authors of the book

10.1   Gerhard Chroust

Gerhard Chroust is an Austrian systems scientist and Professor Emeritus for Systems Engineering and Automation at the Johannes Kepler University of Linz, Austria.
He is the Secretary General of the International Federation for Systems Research (IFSR) and a Board Member of the Austrian Computer Society (OCG). He is an Honorary Member of the Austrian Society for Informatics (ÖGI) and of the Bertalanffy Center for Study of Systems Sciences (BCSSS). Chroust is an authority on formal definition of programming languages, system development processes, software quality standards, process assessment, as well as on human and cultural differences in system development. His current key research is in Human Aspects, Cultural Differences and Systemic Aspects of System Development and Disaster Management, and Representation and Enactment of Software Processes.

1964 he received a Master of Science (Electrical Engineering) from the Technical University, 1965 a Master of Science (Computer Science) from the University of Pennsylvania. In 1975 he was awarded a PhD (Computer Science) from the Technical University Vienna and in 1980 a Habilitation (Computer Science) from the Johannes Kepler University Linz.

From 1966 to 1991 Chroust worked at the IBM Laboratory Vienna. From 1992 until 2007 he was tenured Professor for 'Systems Engineering and Automation' at the Kepler University of Linz.

He has authored 10 books, edited/co-edited approx. 60 proceedings, has written approx. 220 scientific publications and approx. 300 other publications. Since 2007 is a Professor Emeritus of the Johannes Kepler University Linz and continues to do research in the areas of Process Models and their Enactment, Human and Cultural Aspects of Systems Engineering, Human and Systemic Aspects of Disaster Management and Aging.

Chroust is bearer of the Silver Medal of Honor of Upper Austria.

From 1993 onward he was co-chair of the IDIMT Conferences and for most years has also been Co-Editor of the Proceedings.

Website: http://www.gerhard-chroust.at

10.2 Petr Doucek

Petr Doucek is a Czech computing expert with specialization information management and information security management systems. He has graduated in 1984 at University of Economics, Prague in Economic-mathematical modelling. He finished his Ph.D. studies in 1993 and presented a PhD Thesis with Title: "Model Approach to Estimation of Economic Characteristics of Software Projects". He defended successful a thesis "Managerial Applications - EIS in the Czech Practice" and has been appointed Associate Professor in Information Management at the Faculty of Informatics and Statistics at University of Economics, Prague. Since 2007 is Professor for Informatics and since 2010 he is the head of Department of System Analysis.

Topics of his activities are Information Management, Information Systems and Information and Communication Technology, Security Management Systems and Project Management.

He took part in several research activities supported by Czech Funding Agencies as well as by international funds. He participated in more than 35 projects in improvement of information systems in Czech or international firms or in state and public administration bodies.

His rich publication activity consists from eight monographs, 18 education texts, approximately 45 articles in reviewed journals and more than 100 contributions in international conferences and workshops.

From 1993 onward he was co-chair of the IDIMT Conferences and for many years has also been Co-Editor of the Proceedings.

10.3   Lea Nedomová

Lea Nedomová has been working as assistant professor of the
Department of System Analysis at the Faculty of Informatics and
Statistics at the University of Economics, Prague since 1996.
She graduated at the Natural Science Faculty of the Charles
University, with a specialization in Chemistry and Biology.
Her main work areas are system approach to global develop-
ment and sustainable development, especially in relation to ISO
Standard 9000 (Quality Management) and ISO Standard 14000
(Environmental Management). Further fields are sustainability,
IMS, and the use of information in social system, including
a Pedagogic orientation in Office automation systems. Her
main research and development topics include system approach to global society,
sustainable development and its relation to integrated management system and its
components. A further area of her interest is gender aspects of Information technology
implementation and operation.

She is author and co-author of 5 monographs, 18 research articles and 70 papers on
conferences.

Since 2001 she is working as the Organizing Chairperson in the Organizing Committee
of the IDIMT Conferences.